HOW TO

HAGGLE

D1617068

HOW TO

HAGGLE

Professional Tricks for Saving
Money on Just About Anything

Max Edison

PALADIN PRESS • BOULDER, COLORADO

Also by Max Edison:
Beat the Bill Collector
Financial Freedom Now

*How to Haggle: Professional Tricks for
Saving Money on Just About Anythng*
by Max Edison

Copyright © 2001 by Max Edison

ISBN 1-58160-136-0
Printed in the United States of America

Published by Paladin Press, a division of
Paladin Enterprises
Gunbarrel Tech Center
7077 Winchester Circle
Boulder, Colorado 80301 USA.
+1.303.443.7250

Direct inquiries and/or orders to the above address.

Visit our Web site at www.paladin-press.com

Contents

Dedicated to Peanut, gender unknown, estimated date of arrival
September 25, 2000. Daddy can't wait to meet you.
Also dedicated to Frigga, for favors granted.

Chapter One: Why Haggle?

Haggling used to be a time-honored skill. Since the dawn of history, men and women have been have been haggling over the best deal on, well, camels or whatever. Your ancestors–probably farmers or small-town merchants—knew well how to haggle, and their standing in the community partly depended on it. Even today, in Mexico and many other Third World countries, paying sticker price is the mark of a sucker. But not in America.

Americans today, sadly enough, do most of their shopping in terrain unfriendly to haggling, or so it would appear. Wal-Mart doesn't haggle, right? That's what they'd like you to think. If you remember one thing from this book, remember this: *everybody haggles*. Nobody haggles *all* the time, but everybody haggles at least some of the time.

Didn't know that Wal-Mart haggles? I'm not surprised. As a retailer myself, I never go out of my way to tell people they could get a better deal than what I'm offering. Why should I? Think about it. I know that Mexicans, Somalis, and other immigrants who come into my pawnshop will want to dicker. Ditto for old farmers and horse traders. My prices, therefore, are always higher than I expect a customer to pay, just to give myself some elbowroom when bargaining. If someone walks in and pays sticker price, I'm certainly not going to point out his error. And if someone comes in and repeatedly pays sticker price, I'm going to think he's a sucker. I swear, I almost feel guilty sometimes. But it's not my responsibility to make sure they get the best deal.

You may or may not care what a pawnbroker thinks of you. But the fact remains that you could have saved 20 percent—more than $100—on that diamond ring you just bought. If you'd only asked me to "eat" the sales tax, you could've used the savings to pay for a real nice dinner for two.

Lower prices aren't the only benefit of haggling. You can sometimes get extended warranties, additional equipment, and upgrades thrown in for free. You'd really be surprised how far you can push a store owner or salesman for "gimmes" like this. Our standard warranty at the pawnshop is 30 days, "no problems, cash back or exchange." Nevertheless, I've given up to a 90 day warranty, plus connecting cables and whatnot, just to make a sale.

Consider the computer I sold the other day. I was short on cash, having loaned money to everyone else in town so they could pay their rent. A Laotian guy walks in and starts looking seriously at a computer I had for sale. It was an oldie, an IBM compatible 386 that had been upgraded by Lord knows how many kitchen-table technicians. It still had a 5.25-inch floppy disk drive in it, if that tells you anything.

Now realistically, I had *nothing* tied up in this computer. I originally loaned my customer $100 on it, and he more than paid that back in interest before he walked away from it. Sticker price was $350 (Yeah, I know, I'm going to hell, but free market capitalism has those risks).

WHY HAGGLE?

Obviously, I had lots of room to bargain, and because I was short on cash, I might've gone down to $250 or even $200 just to move the thing. Well this guy was no dummy, having come from a haggling culture, and he got me to throw in a free printer (for which I had planned to charge $75). As a haggler, though, he was kind of a lightweight. A Somali (as a culture, among the most accomplished hagglers I've met) probably would've gotten it for $175, plus a free printer, and I would've carried it to the car for him. Still, we struck a pretty good deal and both of us came out ahead.

The bottom line is: if you're not haggling, you're losing money. You can think of the money you save as money you don't have to earn, hence less work you have to do. Alternately, you can think of the money you save as money you *did* earn, tax-free, by knowing how to dicker.

Chapter Two: Who Haggles?

Car dealers. Maybe gun dealers. Creepy guys who set up tables at flea markets. As far as the average person knows, that's about where their haggling opportunities end. As I said in the last chapter, though, *everybody* haggles, even Wal-Mart. Here's a breakdown of some of the best places to use the new skills you're going to learn from this book:

SMALL-TOWN MERCHANTS OR INDEPENDENTLY OWNED STORES

The owner of Jim's Appliance and TV will be much more likely to dicker than a large outlet like Best Buy, but then again he'll have to—Best Buy sells its stuff at about his whole-sale cost. He'll make up the profit margin by servicing what he sells.

HOW TO HAGGLE

In many stores, though, the average sales clerk you stumble across may not be authorized to haggle. Make sure to talk to the owner, or at least the store manager. Getting to know him or her on a first-name basis will almost ensure a good deal every time you come back. As a small-town retailer, I can tell you that repeat customers are our bread and butter, and we'll take a loss once in awhile if we have to just to keep them coming back.

JEWELRY STORES

Just about every jewelry store marks their stuff up 300 to 400 percent, so they've got lots of room to haggle. In my experience, most jewelers will take a 200 or even 100 percent profit rather than lose a quick sale. They seem real stuffy and formal in jewelry stores, but flash the cash and see if they sit up and beg. If not, go to another jewelry store.

PAWNSHOPS AND SECONDHAND STORES

If you can't haggle here, it's time to throw in the towel. Oh sure, you might not have luck dealing with the old ladies at the local hospital thrift store, but in any business operated for profit, you should be able to wrangle a deal. Most secondhand store owners are horse traders from way back, and they'd rather come down a little than lose a sale. In addition, they may only vaguely know what any particular object is worth. If they're asking too much, or if you can make them believe they are, you can probably strike a deal.

CAR DEALERS

Everybody knows you can haggle with car dealers and sometimes get a hefty discount. Just don't fall for the old, "Gee, I'd love to make this deal with you, but my manager says no way, etc., etc." Car dealers haggle best when crappy weather keeps other customers away (nothing like trying to start a car on the dealer's lot at 30 below zero to make sure it'll start for you), near the end of the month (when their sales quotas are due), and from August to September (when the new models are coming out, meaning the older ones are suddenly worth less— what they'd really like to do at this point is sell you last year's model at this year's price).

BANKS

Most people don't know that bankers will cut deals. Bank policy isn't carved in stone. Banks will dicker over percentage points on loans, services like free notary service, and even fees from bounced checks (after all, when they cover one of your checks, what they're really doing is floating you a loan at a tremendous rate of interest).

One of their biggest scams, which is the easiest to decline, is what is familiarly known to bankers as "choke and croak," or death and disability. This is theoretically an insurance policy which will pay your loans should you become disabled or dead. The payments will be no problem, they assure you, as they'll kindly add the price of the policy to your loan (and charge you interest on *that* too).

Realistically, it's an overpriced insurance policy that covers *only* the loan you've just taken out. Think about it—say you've paid off all but $500 of your new car loan, then you become disabled. That pricey insurance policy is going to pay off only that $500. So the farther along you are in your loan, the less it's worth. For the same price, you could get a much more efficient death and disability policy from any insurance agent, maybe one that pays $10,000 no matter what.

Sometimes your banker will say, "You've got to take this policy in order for us to approve the loan." Bullshit. You don't want to pay interest on the money you borrow to pay the policy, *plus* what you're borrowing to pay for the car or whatever. Bear in mind that their product is the loan, and they'd like to see you pay the "sticker price" without quibbling. Again, sometimes you've got to keep going up the chain of command until you find someone who's got the power to say "yes."

CHAIN STORES AND DISCOUNT STORES

Many professional hagglers won't even bother to try their luck at these 800-pound gorillas of the retail world. Discount and department stores like Wal-Mart try to give you the impression that they shoot you their very best price right away, and in many cases they're the benchmark against which others' prices are judged. But even they will cut deals under the right circumstances. Consider the following story.

When my wife and I moved into our new house, we needed a futon bed to sleep on, as our regular bed was full of in-laws. Wal-Mart only had one type of futon, the lousy wood-slat kind, but ShopKo offered three varieties, one of which we wanted. Problem was, they had sold out of all but the display model. I hailed the local minimum-wage lackey and got her to summon the department manager. "Look," I said to him, "we need this couch right now. It's the last one you've got left, and I'll disregard any wear and tear, but I'll need your guys to carry it out to the truck for me, and I want a discount because it's the display model."

"No problem," said the manager, who promptly got two goons to hustle the assembled couch out to the truck. He then proceeded to knock 30 bucks off the price.

INDIVIDUALS WHO PLACE ADS IN THE PAPER OR ON THE INTERNET

Look for the words "best offer" or the initials OBO (which stand for "or best offer"). That tells you these people don't

WHO HAGGLES?

expect anyone to pay the price they're asking, but they're interested in a counteroffer. I always thought that if someone said "best offer" and you offered them a buck, they ought to be forced to take it if no one else came along and offered more. Unfortunately, this doesn't seem to be the case. If you offer someone a price that is grossly under the perceived value, they'll probably just keep the item. Or maybe offer to push your face in.

INTERNET AUCTIONS

Sometimes it's possible to haggle on Internet auctions, but not always. In order to put yourself in the position to haggle, you must be the high bidder, but not a winning bidder, on a particular auction. Hang on, I'll 'splain. Say I'm trying to buy a pre-64 Winchester Model 70, a gun which could easily cost over a thousand dollars. I notice the bidding's going a little slow, so I put my offer in at $800, which is high enough to beat the other bidders, but not high enough to hit the seller's reserve. The seller's reserve is basically a "hidden" price level that needs to be met before he is obligated to sell. If it is not met, he can choose whether or not to sell at the highest bid he received.

So, if you outbid the last guy but do not reach the seller's reserve, the auction ends with no winners. Well now the seller's got a quandary: he went and spent a whole week trying to sell his gun online, and nobody wanted it at his price. He could either a) relist the item on the same or a different auction page, or b) keep the rifle. But wait—here's a bidder who almost came up to his reserve. Maybe he could take a little less for the rifle, and the bidder would pay a little more. The seller contacts the bidder by e-mail and haggling begins.

Now the ball is truly in the buyer's court. During the preceding week, the seller has had a chance to show his rifle before the whole world. The world turned him down. The only people who are going to remember that this guy's got a rifle he wants to sell are the few buyers who already bid on the thing. He can either wait a week (or more—it could be six months before he gets his price for the gun) or take $50 or $100 less than he ordinarily would have and get rid of the thing immediately. It depends on how desperate he is to move it.

Just recently, I had a rifle I'd been stuck with, a Remington 700 ADL chambered for .22-250. My business partner and I had picked the thing up, "as new," for $350 about two years before, and we just couldn't sell the dang thing. I put it up on auction with a reserve of $400, and nobody even came close. Finally the highest bidder contacted *me*. He offered to trade me a Remington 11-87 shotgun, which I knew I could get $500 to $550 out of, for the .22-250, which I couldn't squeeze $400 out of. So while it wasn't instant money, he was offering me something that I *could* turn into instant money, and make a profit at that. Not too shabby.

But his offer wouldn't have done me any good if I hadn't known the value of what he was offering. In this case, since I'm a gun dealer, I knew pretty much right off the bat what I could get for the shotgun. But if you're in unfamiliar waters, you'll want to check around to get an idea of the value of the item in question.

In the next chapter, we'll take a look at how to evaluate the stuff you're bargaining for.

Chapter Three: Testing, Testing

Did you ever throw down a big chunk of cash for something, only to find out later that you paid too much? If you're like me, you got a sick feeling in your stomach and a feeling of resentment toward your new toy. It just wasn't as much fun after you found out you paid $200 too much. Well as a pawnbroker, I get maybe 20 different people trying to sell me stuff every day, and if I guess wrong too often I'm out of business. Since my current job has spoiled me for any real work, I'd have to lie around unemployed while my wife worked two jobs, poor dear. So to preserve domestic tranquility, I've gotta be right at least 95 percent of the time. I boost the odds in four ways.

1. I collect newspaper advertising inserts from the local chain stores. Every time I see something on sale at Wal-

11

Mart or Home Depot, I know it'll be coming through the pawnshop at one point or another. Even if my customer, the seller, paid full price, I'm only going to give him a fraction of the sale price. Wal-Mart or whoever has established the market with their sale price, so that's what my sticker price is based on. When customers ask me why I'm giving them so little for their stuff, I say, "Hey, blame Wal-Mart. Every time they drop prices, I have to keep up with them when I resell stuff. In order to make the same money, I have to pay you less." People seem to understand when I explain things that way.

2. I have a big stack of catalogs that tell me the wholesale and/or retail prices on everything from guns to diamonds to CD players. About two thirds of the stuff I see as a pawnbroker is in those catalogs somewhere. Oh sure, I could just ask the customer how much he paid for his stuff, but we pawnbrokers don't trust *anybody*. That's because people, desperate to get as much as they can out of their stuff, lie to us. If I trust people, I go out of business. If you trust someone's statement that he paid such-and-such for whatever it is he's trying to sell, you're gonna lose money sooner or later. Ask to see the receipt.

3. Now that our shop has full-time Internet access, I check online auctions and classified listings to see what other people are trying to get for the same equipment in similar condition. One of the neat things is that stuff sells so darn cheap on the 'net. I can buy a no-name acoustic guitar from my wholesaler for about $45, then turn around and retail it for $95. But I've actually seen the same guitar on the 'net for $30, which is a double bonus for me. Not only can I quote this wholesale price

to my selling customers, then offer them half of it for their guitar, I can also buy new guitars on the 'net and make an extra $15 profit.

One time I had a guy come in with some graphic design software. He said he paid something like $800 for the stuff. Well, I knew what the resale value on software was (about zero), but just for fun I looked up his software package on eBay. New in box, it was going begging for buyers at $49.99. If you're not researching stuff on the 'net, you're losing money. See the appendix for a listing of websites I've found most useful.

4. I flat-ass guess. I guess based on A) past experience, B) what I think I recall similar stuff is selling for, and C) a price which seems to me to be absurdly low. This doesn't always work as well as it would seem. I once bought a Tasco telescope for $60 after the customer assured me held spent over $250 for the thing. Three months later I saw the same telescope selling new for $100. There's no profit for me at the level I'm into it, so I can either dump it at cost and lick my wounds or take it home and start looking for E.T. I think I'll do the latter.

Then again, I do get lucky sometimes. Once I bought an old, obviously handmade concertina (a musical instrument of the accordion family) for $50 and sold it for $350. Sometimes you get the bear, and sometimes the bear gets you.

Obviously you're probably not going to be looking to buy as large a cross-section of consumer goods as I am. Therefore, your "home library" can probably be quite a bit smaller than mine. You might specialize in cars, in which case you would want to own a copy of the National Auto Dealers Association (NADA) price guide, some issues of a nationwide auto trader publication, and so on. One thing to keep in mind, though, is that the prices quoted are going to be valid *only under ideal circumstances.* If the car's not in the shape it's described to be, or the economy just took a hit, or if it's raining out, or a thousand other things, the price is going to be negotiable.

Here are a few pointers on buying used merchandise, based on my experience. It is important to carefully inspect the merchandise you're looking to buy, and to *know what to look for.* Even if you're not personally concerned with the flaws you find, it's important to point them out. Being able to politely but firmly list them puts you in a much better position to start out with a lowball offer without seeming like a jerk.

GUNS

For God's sake, check the chamber and magazine to make sure it's unloaded before you start fooling around with any firearm! If the seller allows you to play with a loaded gun, it means he's an idiot and deserves to get jerked around on the price. At our pawnshop, we charge $10 for each round the customer leaves in the gun. That is, if somebody comes in with a shotgun with a full chamber and magazine, he gets paid maybe $50 less than he otherwise would have. I've had friends who've put bullets through the walls of gun shops (whose proprietors should've known better), so check that chamber once, twice, and three times.

Guns should be lightly oiled, and all moving parts should move smoothly and easily. Check the area where the butt pad meets the stock to make sure the joint is smooth. If the pad juts out over the end of the wood or plastic (composite) stock, there's a good chance the stock's been cut off, which drops $100 from the value of the gun. Look at the screw holes in the recoil pad to see if anyone's been goofing around with it. They should be perfect, just as the gun came from the factory. Check the heads of the screws that hold the gun together. If they're mangled, that means a "kitchen-table gunsmith" (i.e., an idiot) has been at work, and God knows

14

what problems he's caused. Mangled screw heads are definitely worth a discount.

Look at the metal parts of the gun under decent light. If you see freckles when the light shines off the barrel or receiver, chances are the gun has had light surface rust, which also knocks the crap out of its value. Usually a gun will pick up surface rust when some well-meaning doofus leaves it in the case for 9 months, but fingerprints or atmospheric conditions (the sea air, for example) can cause the same effect. Current or former rust ought to be worth at least a 25 percent discount. At our shop, as far as the NRA grading system is concerned, we downgrade a gun to "poor" condition immediately when we see signs of rust.

Mentally decide what percentage of the bluing and/or wood finish remains. If it's 99 percent, it means the gun looks just like new; 90 percent means 10 percent of the bluing has worn off plus maybe some dings in the stock or some worn-off varnish.

Check the barrel for bulges, warping, or signs of being cut off with a hacksaw. Any one of these can affect the accuracy of the gun (or be a safety hazard) and should probably be the basis for passing on a deal. At the very least, it'll cost you $75 or more to replace the barrel. Look at the inside of the barrel (the bore) under good light. A bore light is ideal, and you can buy one for about $5. Look for rust or excessive wear—either one of these indicates that the gun has either not been taken care of or has had thousands of rounds through it. The bore should be shiny as a mirror, and on rifles and pistols the rifling grooves should be strong and sharp.

Be awful goddamn sure that you know the correct model, grade, and caliber of the weapon you're looking to purchase (or sell for that matter). The price difference between, say, a Winchester Model 1897 standard grade and trap grade can be hundreds of dollars, while the price difference between a Winchester Model 12 shotgun in 12 gauge and one in 28 gauge can literally be thousands of dollars.

HOW TO HAGGLE

I recently spent $575 (including shipping) on an Internet auction for a Winchester Model 101 trap grade shotgun. While almost every variation of the 101 is worth $1,000 or more, there is *one* variation that's only worth $550 or so. That's the single-barrel trap, which I bought without checking closely enough. Looks like I'll be bringing home a shotgun to take out E.T. if I ever locate him with the overpriced telescope I bought in the last chapter.

DIAMONDS

New jewelry is the most grossly overpriced commodity in America today, so it's no wonder that people who are selling think their stuff is, well, made of gold. Jewelers typically mark their goods up 300 to 400 percent, and even when ShopKo or whoever has a 70 percent off sale, they're still making 50 percent or so.

In truth, diamonds are neither rare nor valuable, and the perceived rarity and value is kept in place thanks to a monopoly named DeBeers. You'll remember them from all the warm-and-squishy diamond commercials on TV and in popular magazines.

DeBeers owns over 95 percent of the diamonds and diamond mines in the world and only releases a handful every year. Their chokehold on the world diamond market is such that DeBeers executives are generally not allowed by the company to travel in the United States due to fears that they'll be served with papers for a federal antitrust suit. That being said, let's look at ways to determine the actual value of diamonds.

I can't tell you the number of times that some poor guy has come into the shop with an engagement ring his sweetie has rejected. I ask him what he paid for it. "Fifteen hundred bucks," he says. "Buddy," I say, "I coulda sold you this ring for $600, and I'd have skipped all the way down the street. Wholesale cost on that diamond is about $200, and there's about 12 bucks worth of gold in the setting. As it stands, I'll give you a $100 for it." More often than not, he takes it. What else can he do? The jewelry store won't take it back, and every other pawnshop is going to be quoting him about the same price.

I recently had a guy take me up on my offer. He was a former resident of my area who had moved to Reno, Nevada. "Max," he said, "I'm getting married, and I wanted to make you skip all the way down the street. What can you get me for something in a platinum and diamond solitaire?" I got him a third-carat *certified* (clarity SI1, F-G color—more on this jargon below) diamond solitaire in a platinum setting for $900, which is what most people end up paying for the diamond alone. He called me up later, crowing about how pleased he was with the ring I'd sent him. He wanted to send me more money.

"Don't send me money," I said, "send me more customers. I can do this all day long and make good money."

Oh, I'd love to be a jeweler. They're free to make up wild appraisal values for jewelry without having to pay anywhere near those prices. If someone comes into my shop with a piece of jewelry "appraised" at $1,200, I often ask him if the jeweler was willing to buy it from him for that. Of course not. So all that's left is me and my $100 bid. Who looks like the bad guy? Me, initially, though the more I educate consumers, the better I look.

According to industry brochures, diamonds are graded according to cut, clarity, and color. Cut is easy—you can easily tell an emerald (rectangular) cut from a princess (round) cut or trillium (triangular) cut. But how do you, as an average human being, learn to grade clarity and color? You don't, not without going to a specialized school for a couple of weeks. There are some color grading sets available to which you can compare your diamond, but damned if I feel competent enough to assign a grade. Some gems are certified, which means an independent grading service has looked at the diamonds and graded them, then issued a certificate for future reference. Certified diamonds may be slightly more expensive than uncertified ones, but you may find the peace of mind worth it.

As a diamond buyer, you need to have several tools at the ready (all of which are available from M&M Merchandisers or Moore Sales Co., listed in the appendix):

1. *A thermal diamond tester.* If the rock you're testing is real, it goes "beep" and lights up. If not, it does nothing. This device distinguishes between cut glass or cubic zirconia and real diamonds. It'll cost you about $95, but it'll pay for itself the first time it screens out a bogus diamond.

2. *A moissanite tester.* As if life weren't difficult enough, somebody came up with an artificial diamond that can fool the standard diamond tester. It's called moissanite, and it's usually seen in sizes over half a carat. These have been showing up in pawnshops recently, so somebody has a line on them. A $75 investment in a moissanite tester now could save you hundreds of dollars later. Then again, if you're not looking to buy diamonds of half a carat or more, you probably don't need one (as of this writing, I haven't heard of quarter- or third-carat moissanite pieces being sold).

3. *A sizing gauge.* The size difference between a fifth-carat and a quarter-carat isn't all that great, and you can't always trust your eyes. These gauges are pretty cheap, and they'll tell you the approximate weight of your chosen rock. Hey, it'll cost you $1.95, max.

4. *A 10x magnifying loupe.* Very necessary for looking for black spots (carbon deposits) in the diamond. Also helps you see if the diamond is chipped. Although diamonds are the hardest mineral on earth, they are very brittle.

TESTING, TESTING

Accidentally knocking them against another hard surface or scratching glass with them can chip them. Chipped diamonds are worth *nothing* no matter what the size, as they would have to be recut, which might cost more than the diamond is worth. Then again, nobody without a 10x magnifier can generally tell if your diamond is chipped or not. You could get a helluva discount for buying a chipped diamond that looks great at arm's length.

So, then. You've got your tools, and you've got the diamond in front of you. Test it first with the thermal tester, then with the moissanite tester. Look at it under the loupe to make sure it isn't chipped, then check the size with your gauge.

Diamond size is measured by "points" and "carats." One hundred points equal a carat; thus a 25 point stone would also be called a quarter carat, a 50 point rock would be a half carat, and so on. Generally speaking, diamonds under 15 points are pretty much worthless. I usually pay $25 for a 15 point diamond, maybe $50 or $75 for a 20 point, and as much as $100 or $125 for a 25 point. These prices are about half of wholesale for a pretty good diamond. If you see a lot of black spots under magnification, you might want to pay less.

Beware of TCW, or total carat weight. You might be presented with a ring with a bunch of tiny diamonds on it which the seller says has a total weight of 1 carat. Well, if a 4 point diamond is worth nothing, and you have 25 of them, 25 times zero is still zero, right? I often put it to people this way. Pretend I have two TVs in the shop. One is a standard 27 inch TV, while the other is a 27 inch that has been broken into pieces and glued back together again. Are you going to pay me the same price for the working TV as you would the one that is just a collection of pieces?

OTHER JEWELRY

Other gold and silver jewelry is marked up even more

HOW TO HAGGLE

wildly than diamonds. Your average Black Hills Gold ring, for example, might contain anywhere from $4 to $25 worth of gold, though it originally retailed for $79.95 to $249.95 respectively. In order to evaluate gold and silver, you need:

1. *A digital scale.* Available from M&M or Moore, these pocket-size scales are battery powered and can tell you the exact weight of precious metal. Your dope-dealing friends might have a used one they could sell you.

2. *A 10x magnification loupe.* Helpful, though not necessary. Sometimes the karat value of the gold is extremely difficult to see, and your choices are either to magnify or ruin your eyes.

3. *A knowledge of the recent "spot" price of gold or silver.* This is the price that is listed in the financial section of your local newspaper. It applies only to those who buy 5,000 ounce bars of precious metals at a time; us pikers who buy in lesser quantity are forced to pay a percentage or two above that price. But no matter; the listed price is close enough.

4. *The Rio Grande catalog* (listed in the appendix). This catalog gives nearly wholesale prices for all kinds of precious and semiprecious stones. True story: A gal came into the shop with a string of thin, freshwater pearls. When I asked her what she wanted for them, she replied that a jeweler had said that she might get 75 dollars in a pawnshop. Well, as soon as I heard the word "jeweler" I was on the defensive, but I said, "Let's take a look at what they wholesale for." I opened up the Rio Grande catalog and found the exact same string of pearls wholesaled for about $7.50. I showed this to her and said, "I'll give you ten bucks." She took it.

20

TESTING, TESTING

Unless you can get independent verification from an expert, I would avoid paying extra for any stones that are presented to you as rubies, emeralds, or other precious stones. The problem is that laboratory-created stones are getting to be so perfect that many jewelers can't tell them apart from the real ones. If the stones are really tiny (meaning they're worth nothing), they're probably real. If they look dark and cloudy, they *might* be real. Cheaper stones, like amethyst or onyx, are most likely real, as they're not worth replicating in the laboratory. Here are tests for a few semiprecious stones you might run across:

*   *Turquoise.* Test turquoise by heating up a needle and trying to press it into the stone. Fake turquoise is usually plastic, which will melt.

*   *Pearls.* You can test pearls by rubbing them against your teeth. If they're gritty, they're probably real. Alternately, you could drop one in a glass of vinegar and see if it dissolves. This might cheese off the seller, though, so make sure to get his permission first.

*   *Amber.* Again, heat up a pin and press it into the amber. You should smell a piney smell. If the pin doesn't go in or smells like burning plastic, it's fake.

In this day and age, lots of gold is marked "10k" or "14k," but it's fake, which means it isn't anything but gold plate. Hey, anybody can buy a little stamper that says 10k. I would recommend a gold tester, but unfortunately there's not a decent one on the market. I tried one of the electronic ones, but it seemed unreliable and prone to breakage. The only test I'm aware of that works well is the acid test, which requires damaging the jewelry with a file in order to perform it. Failing a decent tester, we've had to rely on guesswork. Here are some of our rules of thumb for evaluating gold.

One of the ways we test gold is by bouncing it on the

counter. If it makes a tinny sound, it's probably fake. If it makes more of a dull thud, it's probably real. Another good way to tell is to test the attached diamond if there is one. If the diamond is real, the gold is no doubt real. You can also look for the distinctive "leaf" decoration found on Black Hills Gold jewelry. I haven't seen a fake piece yet that has the Black Hills Gold leaves on it.

Another way to help separate junk from jewelry is to use Mr. Magnet. Put a small, portable magnet in your toolbox and test every piece of jewelry with it. While much plated jewelry is gold-plated copper or silver, some of it is plated steel. A magnet is a quick, easy test for plated stuff.

There are a number of gold purity stamps found on jewelry. Here are some of them:

- *14k* means 14 karat gold, or a little over half gold.

- *10k* means 10 karat gold, or a little under half gold.

- *10KE or 14KE* means 10 or 14 karat electroplate, or junk. Since gold can be electroplated as thin as one molecule wide on almost any surface, it stands to reason that such a thin coating is worth nothing.

- *10KP or 14KP* means 10 or 14k *pura*, or pure. It does not mean 10k plate. Anything marked 10KP or 14KP is just fine.

- *10KGE or 14KGE* means 10K or 14K gold electroplate. Like 10KE or 14KE, this marking means junk.

- *417 or .583* is the European standard for marking gold. Seeing .417 means 10k, while .583 means 14k.

- *10KGF or 14KGF* means gold filled, or plate. Long story short, it's junk.

In any case, beware anything stamped or reputed to be made in Mexico. In fact, there's a lot of Mexican jewelry on the market that's marked 10k but ain't. Beware of crudely made jewelry, or anything with the Jesus-on-a-boat-anchor motif. While there is real jewelry available in these styles, it's still a good reason to beware. Any jewelry stamped "Made in Italy" or "Italia" is perfectly good (in fact, it's the industry standard).

For silver, look for the word "sterling" or ".925," which is the percentage of silver in sterling. To a huge extent, if silver is not marked either way, it's not silver. There are itinerant craftsmen in Mexico, or New Mexico, who can't afford the .925 stamp, but they are few and far between. About 99 percent of the time, if something's not marked as silver, it ain't silver.

To evaluate gold, then, set the ring or whatever on your digital scale, then set the mode on the scale to "dwt," which means "dramweight." If the gold is marked 10k, multiply the dwt by .0190, then by the current spot price of gold. If the gold is 14k, multiply by .0266, then by the current spot price of gold. As I write this, the spot price of gold is about $264. Thus, if we have something that weighs in at 2 dwt, 10k gold, we multiply 2 by .0190 by 264 for a total melt value of about $10.03. To evaluate silver, switch the scale to "ozt" (or Troy ounces), then multiply by either .925 (for sterling) or .999 (for fine silver), then multiply by the current spot price for silver.

When evaluating jewelry with stones in it, I usually just pretend the whole thing is 10k or sterling or whatever and punch in the numbers. If the stone is a huge piece of something cheap, like onyx, I might go only half the amount I could get by melting the entire piece, or something like that. You just have to kind of play it by ear.

ELECTRONICS

To evaluate electronics, plug them in and try to make sure

that they do everything they're supposed to. Tape decks should play tapes, CD players should play CDs, and VCRs should play movies without lines or static ("noise"). Many electronic items have their date of manufacture listed on a sticker on the back. Check this date to determine how long you might reasonably expect it to last. Any made-in-China TV that's five years old, for example, is getting close to the end of its useful life.

When testing, be sure to leave the item on for at least 10 minutes. I've tested TVs for five minutes, only to find out I got burned when they overheated after 10 minutes. Likewise VCRs—it seems that almost one in ten VCR has some weird flaw I didn't notice when I first took it in. Check each VCR to make sure it plays, rewinds, fast forwards, and ejects without problems.

Stereo speakers should be hooked up and tested. They should play clearly, without cutting out or getting really distorted at low volume levels. If possible, check the cone of the speaker by removing the grill/cover and make sure that the cones aren't torn or pushed in.

Be especially aware of car audio gear. I fear this stuff because just one bad connection can burn out a piece of equipment forever. Whenever anyone comes into the shop wanting to sell an auto CD or tape deck, I make him go hook it up in his car. If he claims he doesn't know how, I still pass. I've gotten burned on so many car stereos that I don't trust anyone anymore.

Likewise I avoid portable CD players, telephones, and answering machines. Unfortunately most electronics are made in China today, undoubtedly by prison labor, and some things stand up better than others. Every time the big marts drop their prices, quality control follows. I recently sold a 25-year-old TV for $60, and it'll probably last longer than any TV made today.

On the other hand, I've almost never gotten burned on microwave ovens or today's popular game systems (Nintendo 64s or PlayStations). The first generation of PlayStations tend to burn out, but Nintendo 64s do not. Of course, by the time this book hits print, the new systems will be on the market, and their reliability is anybody's guess.

TRENDY COLLECTIBLES

As this book was being written, the Beanie Baby market crashed, depriving would-be hagglers of a year's worth of profits. That always seems to be the way these markets go. Could be Star Wars toys, Cabbage Patch Kids, Tickle-Me-Elmos, or next year's must-have toy, but it seems like the only people who make or retain money on these trendy trinkets are the junk hustlers who are selling them.

While this is not exactly a book about making money buying stuff secondhand, I need to inject a caveat here. If you get hooked on buying the next trendy collectible series that comes down the road, you *will* lose money unless you can sell the stuff to someone who likes the series more than you do. Before the market crashes, that is. Personally, I don't dabble in anything which is really trendy or "collectible." Guns will increase in value over the long haul, and so will coins, but Beanie Babies won't. Okay, electronics decrease in value over the years, but in that field I'm counting on quick sales and being one step ahead of my customers in knowing when the market's gonna crash.

Anyway, if you simply must have trendy items, get yourself a good price guide and make sure the dealers don't jerk you around too much. I wouldn't pay private collectors any more than 75 percent of book (since that's more than any dealer will give them), and I wouldn't pay over full book to a dealer. Better yet, wait 'til the market crashes and buy everything up for ten cents on the dollar. Hey, it might come back in 20 years!

CARS, TRUCKS, AND OTHER MOTORIZED VEHICLES

You can really get burned buying used vehicles if you're

not careful. A friend of mine just took a $9,000 hit in one year on a late-model used car because he didn't know what cars of that make, model, and year were going for. Now he checks eBay to see what it would cost him to pick up a similar vehicle. You could also check out the NADA price guide or the listings in your local paper. This seems like commonsense advice to a lot of us, but my stepbrother, Mikey, is a used-car dealer, and he's told me stories of selling people used cars for more money than their new equivalents.

A lot of people rely on *Consumer Reports* for car information. It's a fine publication for checking on the safety and reliability of a certain product, but it's not worth beans as a price guide. For one, car prices change dramatically (think about the price of a '74 Pinto wagon a day before and a day after the revelation that they burst into flames when rear ended) and vary by region to region in the country. A dealer out in the sticks may be willing to slash his price dramatically when shown that other dealers in larger cities are selling the same car for less. For up-to-the-minute pricing, Internet is the way to go, man.

When it comes to physically checking the vehicle for potential breakdowns, the water gets a little rougher. Obviously you have to go for a test drive, but beyond that, what should you know? When test driving, don't play with the radio—you need to listen carefully to the vehicle and make sure it's not making any funny noises. Let it run in park for 10 or 20 minutes, then check underneath for leaking fluids. Green means coolant, which is usually a couple of hundred bucks to fix; brown/black means oil, which can quite easily cost you a grand; and red means automatic transmission fluid, which should also scare the hell out of you. Check the temperature gauge to make sure the cooling system is working properly. Check the exhaust to make sure it's not burning oil. If smoke is coming out, you're looking at replacing or rebuilding the engine. And those are just the easy points to check.

If possible, you should know a "motor head," a buddy who

knows enough about cars to help you look for serious problems. Pay him a 12 pack of beer or something to check out your potential creampuff. Failing that, find a friendly (honest) mechanic. Many mechanics in my area will go over a vehicle for 30 or 40 bucks, and in my opinion the investment is totally worth it.

Remember that just about any vehicle you buy is going to lose money from the day you drive it off the lot. As you might remember from my book *Financial Freedom Now*, you should never, ever borrow money to pay for stuff that depreciates in value. Think about it: if you borrow money to buy a car, you'll be paying depreciation, full-coverage insurance, a monthly car payment, and possibly (unless it's brand new) repairs. If you get the best car you can afford to pay cash for, you can put minimum insurance coverage on it and possibly pay for some repairs. This approach can save you hundreds on your monthly budget. Both my vehicles are 11 years old, and both are paid for. Neither are going to depreciate a whole lot from where they are right now.

REAL ESTATE

Buying real estate is even worse than buying a car. When my wife and I bought our house, I swore I'd rather yank my teeth out by the roots than go through that whole process again. Nevertheless, we got a pretty good deal. Our house was assessed by the property tax goons at $30,500, the bank appraised it at $40,000, and we paid $35,000. We've since had friends and relatives come in and help with renovations, so I'm guessing it's worth about $50,000 now. We're still getting taxed at the $30,500 rate, though, at least until this book comes out and they find out what we've been up to.

The first thing to do when trying to evaluate a property is to call the local tax assessor, give them the address or legal description, and find out the assessed value. The figure they give you is frequently five or 10 years out of date, but it'll be a nice low figure from an official source. You could pay your own real-estate appraiser to come in and evaluate the property, but as your mortgage lender will be hiring one later (with your money), it would be a waste of money.

In our case, after we got the assessed value and determined between ourselves that we'd pay up to 10 percent more than that, we hired a building inspector. He charged us $300 and went through the entire house, testing outlets and major appliances and looking at the roof and so on. From his report we learned that while the house had no serious problems, the plumbing and wiring were out of date and there was evidence of flooding in the basement. Using this info as ammunition, we proceeded to knock $4,500 off the asking price. Was the house worth what we paid for it? Yes. Was it worth more? Oh my, yes. Three hundred bucks dropped on a housing inspector paid for itself 15 times over.

Of course, if you know someone in the field, you can get a look-over for free. Anybody in the building trades can point out defects within his field (though I wouldn't ask a carpenter to check out the plumbing), and you may save some money doing it. Avoid relying on the expertise of Dad or Uncle Buddy unless they actually do that sort of thing for a living.

And sellers, the thing to do when you're looking to sell is to ask those property tax goons to come through and do a thorough assessment. With any luck your property will have risen substantially in value, and prospective buyers will be willing to pay 10 percent above that value.

What you're really trying to do here is get an official agency to help bolster your inflated asking price. Check out the next chapter for more dirty tricks like this . . .

Chapter Four: Psyching 'Em Out

Haggling is psychological warfare, no doubt about it. Make a slip and you pay too much, or receive too little, for the stuff you're dickering over. Well, there are some unwritten rules to haggling, which a lot of people know, and then there are dirty tricks, which are known only to few.

UNWRITTEN RULES

These are the things your daddy should have taught you but maybe didn't. Most everybody who's any good at haggling knows these rules, and if you break one they get annoyed.

1. Play "hard to get." If a seller can tell that you are in love with an item, he knows he can get his top price. Instead, pretend to be mildly, but not formally, interest-

ed in the piece you're looking at. Don't fall in love, and try not to come back three or four times in the course of the day to look at it. While this shows the seller that you're serious about the item, it also shows him that he can take you for pretty close to sticker price.

2. If you make an offer, that offer stands unless a counteroffer is made. One of the biggest complaints I have about some of my Hispanic, Somali, and other African customers is that I'll have a TV priced at, say, $75. They'll offer $60, and I'll accept, because I can knock 20 percent off the top of anything. Then they'll offer $50, which really cheeses me off and makes me challenge them to put up or shut up.

    Then again, haggling in Mexico is different. Merchants put wildly inflated price tags on their stuff (at least the stuff they want to sell to tourists), then accept, eventually, a price that is 10 percent of that. When my wife Lori and I went to Cancun for our honeymoon, vendors would take off after us if we showed the slightest sign of interest in anything they had to sell. Once, Lori stopped to look at a pair of sandals that the vendor had priced at $40 (400 pesos). While she was only mildly interested in them, he kept coming back, each time with a lower price. "Look," she said every time he came back, "all I've got is 10 bucks. I'm buying gifts for a lot of people, and that's all I can afford to spend." Finally he offered a price of $14. She took it.

3. If you make an offer, you'd better be prepared to pay what you offer. This would be my second big gripe about haggling with the uninitiated. A guy will stand around for 20 minutes talking about an item, then make an offer. If I decline or make a counteroffer, that's okay.

PSYCHING 'EM OUT

But if I accept his offer and he says something like, "Maybe I'll be back Wednesday," I get pissed and he gets no deal, even if he does come back Wednesday.

4. Buyers, if you and the seller can't quite come together on the price of an item, ask him if he's got anything to throw in on the deal. If it's a gun you're haggling over, he might throw in ammo, or a sling, or a gun case. If it's a VCR, he might throw in a couple of free movies. Whatever makes you feel better about paying his final price . . .

5. Never show your whole hand at once. If you're willing to pay $80 for an item, for example, offer $60 (or even $40). You never know—the other guy might take it. Even if he passes or counteroffers, he'll feel like some progress is being made. Sellers, never give your lowest price right off the bat (unless you're desperate to get rid of a piece). Making a firm offer and sticking to it before volleying offer and counteroffer makes the other guy think you're a jerk.

6. Along the same lines, sellers should never let the buyer know how much they paid for an item. If you can buy a Browning Citori shotgun for $88, like I recently did, and sell it for $995, never let the buyer know the price you paid. You could lie, for example, or change the subject. If the buyer knows you paid $88 for a shotgun worth $995 on the open market, he's not going to be inclined to pay you even $300 for it. Why should he? A $200 profit should be enough for any man, right? Wrong. I need all the profit I can get to offset my overhead. Overhead includes rent, busted junk I've bought, wages to my employees, and taxes. Sometimes I make 300 percent profit and it's not enough.

31

HOW TO HAGGLE

7. It's important to nail down beforehand whether sales tax is included or not. Once buyer and seller agree on a price, that price should be solid. Buyers, you should be thinking that the price *includes* tax. Sellers, you should be thinking that the price *does not* include tax. Regardless, this should be hammered out before the buyer reaches for his wallet. Why go through 20 minutes of haggling, only to start the bidding over again when it comes to sales tax?

8. Buyers, always ask for the "cash" price. On the totally innocent level, merchants lose 2 percent or so of the purchase price when a customer uses plastic. They may be willing to take this 2 percent bite if you pay cash. On the illegal level, they may just do this transaction "off the books" and not declare it as a sale. That means nobody pays sales tax.

9. Sellers, for God's sake, back up the quality of your stuff. You might get a dirty little thrill out of screwing somebody with a piece of junk merchandise, but you'll lose their patronage in the future and earn yourself a nasty reputation to boot. To paraphrase what I said before, repeat customers are probably going to be your bread and butter. Don't prove yourself to be a scam artist (and hurting the business of the rest of us) by not guaranteeing the quality of what you sell. I personally guarantee everything I sell (except for car audio, the problems with which I explained earlier), and in the case of diamonds and gold jewelry, I offer to eat the stuff if it's not real. I'd probably do it, too, just to impress a customer.

DIRTY TRICKS

There are certain things you can do that boost your profits or drop your buying price by taking advantage of the other person's weaknesses. Whether these strategies are moral or not is none of my concern. They happen, and you ignore them at your peril. These include:

1. Try to determine how desperate the other party is. One of the first things you should be asking is, "Why are you selling?" If the answer is, "I need the money," you have a sucker on your line. He's just admitted to you that he's desperate to sell. When someone admits that he's desperate, he's also admitted that he'll take a much lower price for what he's got for sale.

    Every day during my job, I deal with people who are desperate—they'll take $100 for a $1200 ring or whatever. If you can determine that the party you're buying from is willing to do *anything* for money, you can rob him of his property. If he doesn't take you up on it today, keep in touch. I always thought that if somebody advertised their car for, say, $1500 or best offer, and I offered a dollar which nobody outbids, I should get the car. Well, you probably won't get that lucky, but if a guy is desperate and he's spent three or four weeks trying to sell his stuff, he may be willing to re-evaluate your offer. About half the time, when I offer someone bottom dollar on his item, he'll walk off in a huff and then come back the next day when he realizes no one else is going to give him any more money.

2. Try to knock the crap out of whatever he's got for sale. Let me put that another way. Nobody likes to be abused or have their stuff abused. Be polite, but point out flaws in the merchandise. If it's got rust or had been rusty, let him know. If the same item goes for a lesser price in your area, let him know. If the item is horribly obsolete, let him know. The fact is, few people really know what

they've got or what it's worth. They know what they *paid* for it, and instinctively they think they want to get about half of that price, but they probably haven't done their research as far as what similar merchandise sells for secondhand. If you can even fake an expertise in the subject, you've got the upper hand (except, of course, if you run into someone who knows more about the subject than you do).

3. Know (or find out) the wholesale price of what he's selling. If the seller paid way too much for his car, rifle, or whatever, it's not your fault. Let him know what wholesale is on the thing. Let's face it; he's got two options: A) he could stick to whatever randomly assigned percentage of retail price that he quoted you, no matter how far off from the real value that might be, or B) he might listen to reason. If the answer is A, there's not a whole lot you can do. When people sell stuff, they often think that stuff is gold, and there's not a whole lot you can do about it. Thank him and politely decline. I've seen so many people trying to sell a Super Nintendo with 10 games for $150 it's pathetic. They have no idea that the current market price for the whole works is approximately $25 (and falling).

  If the seller is willing to listen to reason, show him the price right out of your price guide (one of the books or catalogs mentioned in the appendix) and inform him that the price listed is full retail value for a used piece in excellent condition. At the same time, inform him that you have no intention of paying full retail price. Tell him that if he sold to a dealer he'd be looking at 50 to 75 percent of "book price." Then see if he's willing to dicker. As a pawnbroker, I generally pay 20 to 25 percent of retail value. I'd say about 10 percent of people pass on my offer, but half of them are back the next day, ready to take it when they find no better offer.

4. Tell the seller that you'll go with him to a pawnbroker (or car dealer, or whatever) and see what he's offered for his stuff. Further, you'll pay him 10 percent (or 20 percent, or whatever figure you agree on) over and above what the professional dealer offers him. Since the dealer or pawnbroker is looking to add a fat markup to the offered price (figure 100 to 300 percent for pawnbrokers, and several hundred to several thousand dollars for, say, car dealers), you should have no problem getting a good buy and, at the same time, making your seller happy. Hey, his only other offer was 10 or 20 percent less than yours.

5. Totally fucking lie. The chances are good that the seller really doesn't know how much his stuff is worth, much less what anyone is willing to pay for it. You can tell him that the particular model he's got isn't selling very well, or it has some weird hidden defect, or that Wal-Mart is selling it new for half what he paid (which is not altogether impossible). Whatever story you choose, stick with it and try to get your story straight before he starts questioning you.

    There are some guns on the market, for example, which don't sell well in my area of the country but which sell well in others. If somebody brings in one of these pieces, I'll tell him the first part of that statement but not the last. I'll shoot him a lowball price, and because most of the gun dealers in my area aren't dealing on the Internet, I'll be well within the ballpark of other bids he'll be getting. If I buy it, I'll then immediately put it on the 'net and get top dollar for it.

6. Sellers, you can totally fucking lie, too. When I sell a gun, I take the highest price I can find on the 'net or wherever and quote it to the buyer. If they're buying a new gun, I find the highest price available, quote them 10 percent over that (as our standing policy is 10 percent over cost for new guns), then find the cheapest wholesaler and buy the gun from them. This might net me an extra 5 percent, which does add up over time. There are a dozen hidden flaws you can gloss over in order to get absolute top dollar from the merchandise, from its condition to its desirability.

    Of course, this works both ways—it's always good to have excuses for not paying top dollar, too. One of my favorites is, "Gee, I'd really like to sell it to you at that price, but I've gotta be able to look my business partner in the face." You could substitute the phrase," but I've gotta look out for my bottom line, or else I'm out of business," or "I've got dollars invested, but I'm not willing to take a loss on this," or "These really don't sell well around here."

7. Sellers, always mark your items up about 20 percent or so more than you're willing to take. That way you can appear to "give" a little while not sacrificing your bottom line. Say somebody buys a three-disc bookshelf stereo from me. I'll often throw in three free CDs. Hey, if they're paying sticker price, I'll throw in $6 worth of CDs just to make them happy. And why not? They could've haggled me down 20 percent without any sweat on my part. It's the least I can do to throw in a few CDs, which cost me little to nothing.

8. Whether you're a buyer or a seller, don't trust anyone. One of the key sayings around our pawnshop is one we stole from a car dealer: "Question: How do you know

when a customer is lying? Answer: When his lips are moving." That about sums it up. As a pawnbroker, I get lied to at least half a dozen times a day. I don't take personal offense at it, but I recognize that it happens and I know who's doing it. I used to have a customer who kept coming in for $20 or $30 loans, all the while saying that he had won a sales contest at Electrolux and would be receiving a brand-new Jeep Cherokee shortly. I never saw his brand-new Jeep Cherokee, and you know as well as I do that it never existed, but for some reason he felt the need to lie to me. While I could really care less what this guy did with his life, it was apparently worth it to him to believe that someone else believed that he wasn't a total loser. Whatever—there might be work for budding psychologists here.

Anyway, your buddy Harvey may swear up and down that his VCR works perfectly, but you'll save harsh feelings later by testing his stuff now. Friends are friends, but business is business, and you'll be better off today by recognizing that distinction. In fact, it's come to the point now where I won't lend money to people who I consider to be friends. Doing otherwise leads to weird feelings and strange events overshadowing one's friendships. My friend Tom, for example, started out as a pawn customer but has since had dinner at my house and has been a drinking buddy for some time now. When he came in for a loan on his bike, I loaned him too much. When he failed to make his payments, I ignored it. And when the bike got to sticking around and irritating me with its very presence, I told him to come get it. Could I have pulled his beloved bike and sold it to some gap-toothed stranger? Perhaps, but even I am not that shallow. He got his bike back and never paid me back, but I learned a valuable lesson.

Another buddy—well, a drinking buddy—kept

pawning stuff and never paid me a cent. I wasn't quite close enough to him to give him his stuff back. In fact, I sold it for a profit. But we don't drink together anymore.

On the other hand, buyers, remember that the seller may be telling the truth *as he understands it*. I've had plenty of people through the shop who've either been told by their "significant others" that the jewelry they have is real, or, on a totally insidious bent, who've bought real diamonds only to have them switched by an unscrupulous jeweler. I've had more than one person come in with diamond jewelry that my tester identifies as fake. I know most of these people, and I doubt they're feeding me a line. It seems that somebody, or somebodies, are out there switching diamonds for cubic zirconias. Just another reason to own your own diamond tester. In any case, always test the merchandise without trying to offend the seller.

STUPID MOVES

There are some things that you may have been taught to do which are of no use whatsoever in haggling. It's best to break yourself of these habits before you do any more damage.

The first one is saying, "I've got other people looking at it." Every second-rate haggler seems to think this is a good device to motivate a buyer, and maybe it is—at least a buyer who doesn't know anything about haggling. To a seasoned wheeler-dealer, though, this is a cheap, transparent dodge to try to get someone to buy something he otherwise wouldn't.

I had a kid come in the shop one day with one of those $1500 rings I mentioned earlier. I looked over the ring, then said, "Well, whattaya want for it?"

"Well, Shifty Pete's pawnshop offered me $275 for it," he said.

"Oh, you'd better take them up on it," I said, "I'm not gonna come anywhere near that."

"How-how much will you give me?" he stammered.

"The most I could do would be a hundred bucks," I said. He took it.

The kid bluffed, hoping I'd want to come close to or beat the theoretical offer from my competitor. I called his bluff because I really didn't need another quarter-carat diamond ring sitting around and gathering dust (plus, I recognized the form of the "I've-got-someone-else-looking-at-this" dodge). Well, he lost, and what I could've done, if I was feeling cruel, was to say, "Oh, I think you better run that ring back to Shifty Pete's. I couldn't rip you off for $175," then watched him squirm. But I'm not in business to expose people's lies. I took it for $100.

Another stupid move is knocking apart the merchant's wares or feigning disbelief. Nothing gets my dander up quicker than when I feel I'm slyly or overtly being accused of selling overpriced junk. It makes me get all defensive and refuse to invest any time in the haggling process. While I recognize that my merchandise is usually not showroom new and that my pricing is sometimes guesswork at best, it doesn't pay to be rude about it. You can gently inform me of things, like the used telescope that I've got marked at $200 is selling new for $100, but to rant and rave and make a production out of it makes me not want to do business with you.

While you want to get the seller to come down on price, it's better to do it in a way that can make him feel good about himself, too. If you say something like, "Hey, y'know what those sell for new, don't ya," he'll say, "What?" and you can tell him or show him a flier where the price is listed. He'll feel sheepish, but he'll still want to make the sale, so his asking price will go down 25 percent or so below the price listed in the flier. He'll also be grateful to you for being such a good sport about his blunder, so you'll have a better chance of getting an instant deal next time. Not *that's* using psychology.

Chapter Five: When and Where to Haggle

While we've learned that everybody haggles, I haven't yet shown you *how* people haggle differently under different situations. Someone who needs the money today may not haggle very long at all. Indeed, he may take your first offer. On the other hand, someone like me who owns his own shop may not be quite so desperate. In addition to location, other factors may cause people to haggle more or less than they otherwise would. In this chapter, we'll take a look at what makes people haggle in different ways at different times and how you can take advantage of it.

The two main factors that motivate people to haggle more (or not at all) are A) time, and B) attachment to the item. I'll explain.

I have a pawnshop that is open approximately 300 days per year (give or take, depending on holidays and whatnot). In addition, I have Internet access so that I may put my wares in front of the entire world. Aside from becoming a small version of Wal-Mart, which is open 24 hours a day in my area, I'm putting my goods in front of as many people as I possibly can.

Now consider the opposite end of the spectrum. I'm a homeowner who's having a garage sale. I've only got one or two days, and whatever doesn't sell then is going to plague me for the next year. I may or may not have Internet access, and I may or may not be interested in selling stuff on the 'net (assuming I know how). Now which one of us do you think is going to hold out for sticker price, and which of us is going to take a huge price cut just to dump his stuff?

I would almost make the sweeping statement that you can always haggle more with the person having the garage sale, but sometimes you have to deal with emotional attachment (e.g., "this was Grandpa's rocker") or a wildly inflated sense of value ("I paid $1200 for this ring, and there's no way I'll take less than $600"). Well whatever, lady. I couldn't get $400 out of the thing if I had it on display in my store, but some angel is gonna pay you $600? Lotsa luck.

If someone won't part with his stuff for a reasonable price (that is, let you steal it), you're better off looking elsewhere. In my vast garage sale experience, it seems like upper middle class or wealthy people often give the best deals. They know what the piece is worth alright, but they view it as just laying around, cluttering up their lives. People who have less money, in my opinion, are more likely to have wildly inflated ideas about what their stuff is worth. Someone, sometime, told them that their silver-plated serving set was "worth money," and they've never let go of that idea in their lives of quiet desperation. However many of their possessions they lose, there's always "grandma's silver" to fall back on. People who give them an honest, frank appraisal of what grandma's silver is actually worth may as well be talking Swahili—the sellers automatically assume that you're deluded or lying and clutch the silver-plated stuff all the tighter.

My favorite example of running into someone with no time and no opportunity to sell is being approached by someone in a bar (or, in my case, a pawnshop). Their baby might need diapers, or they might need to pay the phone bill by the next day, or whatever. All that matters to you is their desperation. These people will likely take any offer bordering (and I do mean bordering) on reasonable. You might pay $20 to $100 for a shotgun, for example, or $50 for an almost new CD deck. On the other hand, maybe one of the reasons they want to get rid of the thing is because it's a piece of junk. Test thoroughly.

Any time I shoot a pawn customer a wildly low figure for his item and he leaps at it, I know to be careful. Most people really aren't all that clever about lying, so their reaction makes me test things even more than I otherwise would.

If they leap at the price and the stuff tests out, hey, maybe it's stolen. It's up to you whether you want to handle stolen stuff or not. Some people don't care, but I cooperate fully with local law enforcement in my pawnshop. This is less a moral choice than a practical one (though I think stealing someone's stuff *without* their permission is wrong). If I buy stolen stuff, I'm helping a thief participate in his livelihood of choice. How long, as he practices, will it take him to break into *my* house and steal *my* stuff? As a "Big-L" Libertarian, I'd rather see him locked up and deal with (relatively) honest people instead.

On the other hand, if a seller seems pained to take such a low price for his valuable property and takes his time (five minutes or so) thinking about it, the chances are pretty good that the stuff is legit. Either that or the seller is a consummate actor. If you keep dealing with the same people, you'll learn whose stuff is generally good and whose is junk.

Anyway, back to time and opportunity. I, as a retailer and e-tailer, have (as I view it) unlimited time and opportunity, and I *really* hate to lose money on an item. I'll sit on a piece for a year before I lose a dime on it. Therefore, I'll allow myself to get haggled down to my point of minimum profitability, then haggle no more.

On the other hand, I as a retailer do have overhead to pay, which a garage sale seller doesn't. Every month I need to pay rent, utilities, wages, and credit card bills, and I still need to be able to loan money out or to buy other people's merchandise. If you look around and see that my shop is full of treasures and it's just before or after the beginning of the month, the chances are good that I can stand to make a sale. At these times I'll dip below my usual point of profitability just to free up some of the money I've got tied up in inventory.

If you're trying to sell me stuff, don't expect a premium price at these times. The times I really need to buy stuff are when my shelves are empty (almost never), before Christmas, and when people get their income tax checks. Other than that, I've still got plenty of time and opportunity to buy stuff from other people, and I can pretty much pick my price.

You can get a little more money, though, by making sure that your stuff is clean and in good working order. Electronics should come with remote controls, manuals, and necessary cables. Microwaves should be clean, not encrusted with food. Leather coats should have liners and working zippers. Guns should be unloaded, rust-free, and recently cleaned. You get the idea.

Another thing you can do is dress up a little. I see so many customers who come in unshaven, sweaty, and with a beer gut poking out of their T-shirt that I really pay attention when somebody well-groomed and well-dressed comes in to sell something. Fair or not, my perception is that the well-groomed customers (in other words, the ones who don't look like they need the money) are the ones to whom I'm going to have to give a better purchase price. In fact, there have been studies done where well-groomed people and poorly groomed people were set up to sell identical items in the same pawnshop. In more than 80 percent of the cases, the neater person got more cashola.

And sellers, please, pick your selling time to maximize profit. Neither I nor anyone else needs to buy an air conditioner in October, nor do we need to buy leather jackets in July. I get a lot of people trying to sell me nonseasonal stuff, and I keep turning them away. "Dude," I say, "*nobody's* buying fur coats in July. Come see me in December." In December, of course, they decide they need the fur coat more than they need the money and keep it through the next spring. The cycle repeats.

On the other hand, there's no time when I'm more desperate to *sell* a leather jacket than in July. This seasonal merchandise problem can lead to big savings for buyers who are capable of thinking three months ahead. Oh sure, I could think three months ahead, too, and make super profits on fur coats I bought in July. But I'm just in this business to make a buck, not necessarily to provide myself with more inventory. I can triple or quadruple my money every month if I buy the right stuff, so sitting on seasonal merchandise pretty much represents a loss as far as I'm concerned.

Anyway, my whole point here hearkens back to the point where I told you, "Ask why the seller (if not a retailer) is selling the item." If he says, "My wife is pregnant and we really need the money," you know he's got neither time nor opportunity and he'll probably take a price hit on his Chevy. If he says he's just bored with it and is thinking about getting something else, chances are he's not quite bored enough to get raped on the price.

And herein lies a lesson to you sellers: never let them see you sweat. If you show fear or desperation, buyers will be gnawing on your bones like rats within 10 minutes. If you really are desperate or don't have too many chances to sell your piece, you're better off to keep a stony look on your face and totally fucking lie about it.

HOW TO HAGGLE

Here's a quick rundown on where you might find haggling opportunities and special things to keep in mind.

GARAGE SALES

The seller undoubtedly paid full retail price for everything he's trying to sell, and no matter how old his stuff is, he feels that a fair resale price is half what he paid. If, however, at the end of the day he hasn't sold a particular piece you are interested in, he could loosen up considerably. He generally claims that all his stuff works, though he may not have had it plugged in and working for 10 years. Merchandise is often dirty, stained, ripped, and frayed. Important pieces may be missing. All of this is fodder for dickering in your favor.

And how's the return policy at a garage sale? Not exactly ironclad.

FLEA MARKETS

Most vendors at flea markets are there because they have nothing else to do that summer. They'll be retirees, officially classified as "disabled," or whatever. They're usually not real desperate to sell any of their stuff since they're probably getting a decent trade from tourists. Plus, they know more about haggling than you do. They probably picked up most of their inventory from other folks coming by the flea market at a hefty discount, so they have room to move—they just don't want to. They don't particularly need the money, so they don't want to sell it for a penny less than the price they saw in a book somewhere.

Flea market vendors probably will take returns on non-functional merchandise, but only if you drive all the way back up north, tourist boy.

WHEN AND WHERE TO HAGGLE

PAWNSHOPS

These are kind of like indoor flea markets that keep regular business hours. The same warnings apply, but you can generally motivate the proprietors by appealing to their sense of greed. Merchandise should be clean and in decent repair, but make the proprietor plug in and test anything you're thinking about buying from him. Rings purported to contain diamonds should make the thermal diamond tester go beep.

Any decent pawnshop will have at least a 30 day return policy, but keep your receipt.

REGULAR RETAIL STORES

It may have been so long since the manager got haggled on that he may give in due to shock. Don't expect a huge discount, but you can usually trim 10 or 20 percent off the asking price if you come up with a good enough reason (like buying an air conditioner in October). Many times mom and pop stores will try to match their competitors' sale prices or throw in enough freebies to make it worth your while, but you'll need to ask. Merchandise is obviously new in the box, except for display items, and often comes with a manufacturer's warranty.

The return policy is generally excellent.

CAR DEALERS

They're like pawnshops that sell cars. It's awfully damn tough to get the upper hand from a car dealer, as they've forgotten more about the trade than you've ever learned. Plus, they're under constant pressure to sell, so many of them will say *anything* to get your name on the dotted line. If it's a "buy here, pay here" lot where they arrange the financing, expect a whole new round of haggling just when you thought you were done.

HOW TO HAGGLE

Beware of "bird dogs"—people who are paid by the dealership to recommend it to their friends. For every paying customer they send in, they might get a $100 bill, or they might get (often fictional) savings on future purchases from that dealer.

You get the best deals just before the end of the month, when many salesmen are desperate to make their quota (or they lose their jobs). Also try during bad weather (rain, blizzards) and just after the next year's models come out.

Return policies vary, but many states do have "lemon laws" that say that the dealer has to take the car back within a certain period of time if it's unrepairable or is constantly breaking down.

AUCTIONS

There's no haggling at auctions, just a sudden death, who's-got-more-money type of feeding frenzy. It's easy to lose your shirt at an auction—all you have to do is get caught up in the bidding war. You can also get some great deals at auctions, since your only competition is other bidders, who may or may not know more about the merchandise than you do. We go to a lot of gun auctions, and it's been my experience that a piece either goes way too cheap or old farmers bid the crap out of it, paying much more than fair retail price. Show up early so you can carefully examine the lots you're interested in. Bid? Don't bid? You've got three seconds to decide.

Return policy? Forget it.

SALES ON THE STREET

This doesn't happen much in my small Minnesota town, but you big-city denizens will sometimes run across a stranger who wants to sell you jewelry or household goods out of the trunk of his car.

Be afraid. Be very afraid. You shouldn't buy jewelry, household goods, or stereo stuff off the street for the same reason you shouldn't buy drugs off the street—you just don't know what you're getting. Now doubtless this guy will have a pretty good story (after all, his income depends on it), but the stuff is almost certainly junk or stolen, two categories of items you don't want to end up with.

As for returns? Three minutes after he takes your cash, he's down the road, never to be seen again.

ONLINE SALES AND AUCTIONS

Millions, nay, billions of dollars are trading hands over the Internet, which is (at the time of this writing) tax-free. While I've had a few bad experiences trading over the 'net, I still consider it well worth my while to do as much business there as possible. Prices are generally lower than retail, a seller's honesty can be reckoned by his "feedback," and payment can be transferred using a credit card or payment services such as e-gold or PayPal.

While I've found that most people I've dealt with on the 'net have been scrupulously honest, there does seem to be the problem that you're dealing with amateurs. I've had guns show up that were reblued/refinished (which knocks the heck out of their value), rusty, or otherwise not in the condition I thought I was paying for. Then again, I've sent money off and never gotten anything. Try to ask as many questions about the piece as you can before you actually pay for it, and get pictures if possible.

Return policies vary, but some sites (like www.auction-arms.com) set a mandatory three-day inspection as part of the terms and conditions of doing business on their site. Some sites have no such rules. I'll never knowingly buy a gun without a three-day inspection period, but I may buy other things like comic books or CDs on an "as is" basis.

HOW TO HAGGLE

REAL-ESTATE SALES

Realtors are punks who know how to present real estate in the best possible light. They are at the beck and call of sellers who know nothing about presenting real estate in the best possible light and who are wildly emotional about any new development, since this is the biggest monetary deal most of them will make in their lives. Be glad you get to deal with the Realtor. Just remember, the Realtor works for the seller. He is their hired lackey, and his job is to get the highest possible price for the property. Any haggling you do will be with the sellers, via the Realtor, who takes all the emotion out of his side of it.

Of course, you can have your own lackey, too. There are creatures called buyer's agents who basically act like a Realtor in reverse. Sometimes Realtors themselves act as buyer's agents. My thoughts at this time are that buyer's agents are not really necessary, since the buyer wields most of the power anyway. Does the seller want to come down to the offered price, or does he want to pay taxes on his empty house for another year? As far as the buyer is concerned, there's another house for sale right down the street. Sooner or later he'll get what he wants at a good price. The seller, in my opinion, cannot afford to be that cavalier.

People sell their houses for all sorts of reasons, and while many of them will undoubtedly want to sell theirs quickly, real estate sales are burdened with emotion on both sides, which may make coming to terms difficult. Further, sometimes the real estate is owned by a corporation, in which case you're at the mercy of whatever faceless bureaucrats think the property ought to be worth.

Return policy? Fuhgeddabowdit!

Chapter Six: Putting it All Together

Now that you've got a decent understanding of what's required to strike a deal, we'll run through a few examples here to show you how everything fits together.

SCENARIO ONE

A guy at work says he's got a couple of guns he needs to get rid of. Apparently his wife got too nervous about the kids getting hold of them. Your ears perk up, since he's already as much as admitted that he's desperate to get rid of them.

"What do you think you'll need to get for 'em," you casually ask him.

"Oh, I know what they're worth [*he doesn't; he knows what he* paid *for them—Max]*, but I'll never get 500 bucks for 'em. I guess I'd go 300 for the pair, cash.

"You don't happen to know the manufacturer and the model numbers, do you?"

He doesn't but agrees to bring the guns to work the next day so you can take a look at them.

The next day comes and you look at the guns. They seem to be in pretty good shape; not like new in the box, but maybe 95 percent. You politely point out the minor dings to him, then carefully jot down the makers and the model numbers, then thank your buddy for his time.

"You bet," he says, "but just get back to me as soon as you can. There're a coupla other guys lookin at 'em."

You briefly wonder if he stayed up all night thinking of that "other buyer" approach but promise to get back to him the next day.

After checking your price resources, you determine that fair retail value for his two guns ought to be about $350. While that's more than he's asking, it's not substantially more. You decide to offer him $200. That night you remove all cash from your wallet except a few fives and ones.

When you see him at work, you call him over. You tell him that the guns are worth what he's asking but that you can't afford that price right now (even if you can). Instead, you pull two $100 bills out of your pocket and thrust them in front of his face. He wavers, again citing the phantom "other buyer." You dig through your wallet, pretending to see what you can add to the offer. You add $18. He takes it. Done deal.

SCENARIO TWO

You see a classified ad for a particular type of car that you're in the market for. You call the number, verify the guy's still got the car, and make an appointment to see it. Since you've been watching the classifieds for awhile and doing some price checking on the Internet, you pretty much know the price range you're willing to pay.

PUTTING IT ALL TOGETHER

When you get to the seller's place, you greet him and he shows you the car. You notice immediately that it's been freshly washed, waxed, and detailed. While you know that this attention doesn't really add any value to the vehicle, it sure does help it sell.

You check the car carefully while it's running, then take it for a test drive. It seems to be in great shape. You ask the seller what he wants for it.

"Forty-five hundred," he says, "or best offer."

That seems a little high to you. The last car you've seen similar to this one cost about $500 less. "Well," you say, "I'm gonna offer you $3500 for it, and I hope that'll be the best one."

The seller points out all the car's best features again and says he might come down a hundred bucks or so. You respond that you might come up a hundred dollars or so but that you think you're too far apart to make a deal. You shake hands and part amicably.

Two or three weeks later, you notice his ad is still listed in the paper. You call him again and reintroduce yourself, reminding him of your offer. This time he takes it, having assured himself that just about everybody who wanted to look at the car had already done so. Done deal!

SCENARIO THREE

You're in a pawnshop looking for a diamond for your sweetie. You see the store has a half-carat rock on display. The listed price is $700. You ask the proprietor over and indicate that you'd like to look at that rock a little closer. He pulls it out (the diamond, that is) and starts telling you what a fine piece of jewelry it is. You listen to what he says but don't necessarily believe him. You ask him to pull out his diamond tester and prove that the rock is real. He does so. Then you ask him to check it on the moissanite tester. He does so.

"Do you have a loupe?" you ask. "I'd like to check it for chips and cracks."

He produces one.

When you look at the diamond, you don't see any chips or cracks, and there seem to be a minimum of black spots. The rock looks kind of dull, but you're not sure whether that's due to it being dirty or it being a bad cut. You point this out to the proprietor. He shrugs.

"I'll offer you four hundred for this diamond," you say. If he takes that price, you'll be stealing it from him.

"'Noooo," he says, "I've got more than that into it. I'd take six fifty." You're pretty sure he's lying, but you counteroffer.

"Five hundred," you say, "and not a penny more."

"Six hundred," he says. "Flat—no taxes."

"I hadn't intended on paying any," you say. "Five hundred and you can keep the setting; I'm having the diamond reset anyway."

"Five fifty, and you're robbing me," he says.

"Done," you say.

As you can see, haggling is a skill that must be practiced. There's no scenario I can show you that will cover every situation. Keep the rules in mind, do your research, and you'll come out fine. Oh, and remember: you'll never *lose* money by passing on a deal.

Appendix: Sources for Tools and Prices

Some of the companies listed here only want to do business with wholesalers (marked with a *). If you know someone who's got a retail business, you might convince him to have the catalogs sent to his place. Otherwise, you can call the companies below and lie.

INTERNET SOURCES

eBay. Most people have heard of this site; real-world prices for coins, comics, antiques, diamonds, etc. Basically everything but guns. (www.ebay.com)

Auction Arms. Features real-time auctions of guns and gun-related items. (www.auctionarms.com)

Guns America. This site lists classified ads for guns and gun-related items. Prices are usually top dollar. (www.gunsamerica.com)

Gun Broker. Another gun auction site set up much like eBay. (www.gunbroker.com)

The Tulving Company. Gives free daily bullion spot quotes and sells gold and silver coins at wholesale prices. (www.tulving.com)

Motley Fools. While they don't give wholesale info, there are a couple of great articles on this site pertaining to home and car buying. (www.fool.com)

Edmund's. A great place to go for determining used car values. (www.edmunds.com)

Kelly Blue Book. Another great source for determining new and used car prices. (www.kbb-com)

REAL-WORLD COMPANIES

M&M Merchandisers. * 1923 Bomar Ave., Fort Worth, TX 76103-2102. These guys offer a wide selection of electronics, plus jewelry supplies and musical instruments.

Wholesale House. * 503 West High St., Hicksville, OH 43526. Another car and home audio wholesaler. Also sells telephones, boom boxes, car alarms, etc. I use this catalog a lot for pricing used car audio equipment.

Moore Sales Co. * 11 Gilbert Rd., Burkburnett, TX 76354. These guys carry much the same product line as M&M Merchandisers.

APPENDIX: SOURCES FOR TOOLS AND PRICES

Gun List. Published by Krause Publications, 700 E. State St., Iola, WI 54990-0001. This is a classified listing publication for guns and gun-related items. Some dealers really hate having the general public get their hands on this information. At $36.98 per year, it's a must-have for gun lovers.

Rio Grande. 7500 Bluewater Rd. NW, Albuquerque, NM 87121-1962. These folks sell jewelry and gems to the public at prices that seem to be just above wholesale. In fact, they've even beaten my wholesaler on platinum prices.